HOMELAND SECURITY
OPERATIONAL ANALYSIS CENTER

Securing U.S. Elections

A Method for Prioritizing
Cybersecurity Risk in
Election Infrastructure

QUENTIN E. HODGSON, EDWARD W. CHAN, ELIZABETH BODINE-BARON,
BRYAN BOLING, BENJAMIN BOUDREAUX, BILYANA LILLY, ANDREW J. LOHN

This research was published in 2022.

Preface

This report describes a methodology for prioritizing cybersecurity risk in election systems in the United States. In 2018, the U.S. Department of Homeland Security's (DHS's) Cybersecurity and Infrastructure Security Agency asked for analytic support to develop a national view of risk in election systems to aid in providing timely and targeted assistance to state and local election officials. This report reflects analysis conducted from August 2018 to August 2019. It should be of interest to election officials, cybersecurity professionals, and researchers examining cybersecurity risk in election systems.

This research was sponsored by the National Risk Management Center, a division of the Cybersecurity and Infrastructure Security Agency, and conducted within the Strategy, Policy, and Operations Program of the Homeland Security Operational Analysis Center (HSOAC) federally funded research and development center (FFRDC).

About the Homeland Security Operational Analysis Center

The Homeland Security Act of 2002 authorizes the Secretary of Homeland Security, acting through the Under Secretary for Science and Technology, to establish one or more FFRDCs to provide independent analysis of homeland security issues.[1] The RAND

---

[1] Section 305 of Public Law 107-296, as codified at 6 U.S.C. § 185.

Corporation operates HSOAC as an FFRDC for DHS under contract HSHQDC-16-D-00007.

The HSOAC FFRDC provides the government with independent and objective analyses and advice in core areas important to the department in support of policy development, decisionmaking, alternative approaches, and new ideas on issues of significance. The HSOAC FFRDC also works with and supports other federal, state, local, tribal, and public- and private-sector organizations that make up the homeland security enterprise. The HSOAC FFRDC's research is undertaken by mutual consent with DHS and is organized as a set of discrete tasks.

The results presented in this report do not necessarily reflect official DHS opinion or policy.

For more information on HSOAC, see www.rand.org/hsoac. For more information on this publication, see www.rand.org/t/RRA512-1.

Contents

Figures and Tables

Figures

Tables

Summary

Addressing cybersecurity risk in election systems is an important initiative requiring partnerships across federal, state, and local governments and with the election system vendor community. Since then–Secretary of Homeland Security Jeh Johnson declared elections a subsector of critical infrastructure in January 2017, the U.S. Department of Homeland Security has engaged state and local election officials to provide cybersecurity services and products to improve their cybersecurity posture. These services have included assessments to identify vulnerabilities in public-facing websites, conducting tabletop exercises, creating outreach products for state-level officials to engage with their local-level counterparts, promoting cyber information sharing and collaboration, and deploying network monitoring and intrusion detection systems.[1]

The election system in the United States is, in reality, not one system, but a tapestry of many different systems. Although they all encompass the same functions, system processes and infrastructure vary from state to state and often between jurisdictions within a state. This report provides an overview of the methodology that researchers from the Homeland Security Operational Analysis Center developed to prioritize risk in election systems in the United States.

The risk prioritization method presented in this report addresses components of the election system that are under the control or are the responsibility of state or local election officials. It is intended to provide a high-level view of relative risk across election system com-

---

[1] Cybersecurity and Infrastructure Security Agency, "Election Infrastructure Security," last revised May 13, 2020.

ponents. It does not address election cybersecurity risk to candidates, political campaigns, social media platforms, or other aspects of elections not under the direct control of election officials. Nor does it address disinformation or influence campaigns regardless of whether such efforts use digital media. It is important to note as well that the risks we assessed are direct cybersecurity risks—that is, the potential risks of a cyber attack on a component of the election system. This risk prioritization method does not *directly* measure the secondary or tertiary effects of such attacks, such as the potential for loss of public confidence in the election process. The methodology covers the main components of election infrastructure in the United States and is intended to assist election officials in understanding and prioritizing risk and in taking steps to mitigate the greatest risk, where possible.

Elections are not simply about voting. Other processes must function to enable people to vote and to ensure that those votes are counted and reported. Consequently, in our analysis, we examined the following components of the election system:

- voter registration
- pollbooks
- voting machines
- tabulation
- official websites.

In our assessment of election systems, we considered different types of attacks across these election system components. An adversary might seek to compromise election infrastructure to accomplish different goals. We distinguish three types of attacks on each election infrastructure component using the "CIA triad" commonly used in cybersecurity: confidentiality attacks, integrity attacks, and availability attacks.

We evaluate risk as a function of likelihood and consequence. Given the challenges in assigning probabilities for each cyber attack as traditional risk assessment methods prescribe, in our methodology, likelihood is determined based on the level of sophistication an adversary would require to successfully attack an election system component, given the security controls in place. Consequence is determined based on the scale of an attack's effects, paired with a rating of severity of that attack in terms of the way it would impede election officials' ability to continue to carry out their duties and conduct an election.

To provide a risk score, we calculated the product of the numeric representations of capability (likelihood), scale of attack, and severity. Although this product provides a single numeric value for risk, there is no standard interpretation for this value on its own. In other words, a risk "score" of 32, for example, should not be interpreted as having a specific value or importance except in terms of allowing us to differentiate relative risks.

The approach to evaluating risk in election systems in this report is intended to provide a first step in a risk assessment but not to replace more-detailed analysis and assessments, such as identifying potential vulnerabilities or misconfigurations in the specific technology an election official oversees. The risk prioritization can not only point to where risk lies but also highlight areas in which election officials can seek assistance from others.

Acknowledgments

For their support and engagement, we wish to thank Matthew Masterson, Geoff Hale, Robert Hanson, Ryan Macias, Seth McKinnis, Eric Rollison, Heather Scott, and Allison Snell, who, at the time of this project, were all with the Cybersecurity and Infrastructure Security Agency. We also thank the numerous election officials and members of the broader election community who participated in workshops and webinars and gave freely of their time to provide insights and critique analysis stemming from the methodology laid out in this report. We thank our reviewers, Jennifer Kavanagh, Thomas F. Atkin, and Anu Narayanan, all from RAND, for their detailed reviews and critiques. We could not have done this without strong support from Homeland Security Operational Analysis Center leadership: Lara Schmidt, Henry H. Willis, and Terrence Kelly. Finally, none of this would have been possible without Erica Robles' and Stephanie Bingley's tireless work.

Abbreviations

ATT&CK	Adversarial Tactics, Techniques, and Common Knowledge
CISA	Cybersecurity and Infrastructure Security Agency
DHS	U.S. Department of Homeland Security
EAC	U.S. Election Assistance Commission
EI-ISAC	Elections Infrastructure Information Sharing and Analysis Center
FFRDC	federally funded research and development center
HAVA	Help America Vote Act
HSOAC	Homeland Security Operational Analysis Center
IPS	intrusion prevention system
MFA	multifactor authentication
NIST	National Institute of Standards and Technology
VRDB	voter registration database
WPA	Wi-Fi protected access

CHAPTER ONE

Introduction

Concern about cyber threats to election systems in the United States gained particular prominence in the 2016 presidential election. The Secretary of Homeland Security and the Director of National Intelligence issued joint statements in October and December 2016 accusing the Russian government of engaging in malicious cyber activity to interfere in the U.S. election.[1] The scope and extent of Russian activity may never be fully known, but that activity included targeting multiple components of the election system across numerous states and counties, as well as engaging in widespread disinformation campaigns.[2] Despite irregularities identified in some jurisdictions, though, federal authorities have yet to find definitive evidence that the cyber targeting of U.S. election infrastructure materially affected the outcome of the election.[3] The United States is not the only country to be affected, either. The cybersecurity firm FireEye identified cyber threat activity related to elections in more than 15 countries between 2016 and 2019.[4]

---

[1] U.S. Department of Homeland Security (DHS), Office of the Director of National Intelligence, and Federal Bureau of Investigation, "Joint DHS, ODNI, FBI Statement on Russian Malicious Cyber Activity," December 29, 2016. See also Office of the Director of National Intelligence, National Intelligence Council, *Assessing Russian Activities and Intentions in Recent US Elections*, Intelligence Community Assessment 2017-01D, January 6, 2017.

[2] Kim Zetter, "How Close Did Russia Really Come to Hacking the 2016 Election?" *Politico*, December 26, 2019.

[3] Our discussion in this report focuses on cyber threats to election infrastructure, so we did not assess the impact of broader influence operations. More on this later.

[4] FireEye, *Cyber Threat Activity Targeting Elections*, Milpitas, Calif., 2019.

Addressing cybersecurity risk in election systems is an important initiative requiring partnerships across federal, state, and local governments and with the election system vendor community. Since then–Secretary of Homeland Security Jeh Johnson declared elections a subsector of critical infrastructure in January 2017, DHS's Cybersecurity and Infrastructure Security Agency (CISA) has engaged state and local election officials to provide cybersecurity services and products to improve their cybersecurity posture. These services have included assessments to identify vulnerabilities in public-facing websites, conducting tabletop exercises, creating outreach products for state-level officials to engage with their local-level counterparts, promoting cyber information sharing and collaboration, and deploying network monitoring and intrusion detection systems.[5] CISA has also contracted with the nonprofit Center for Internet Security to establish the Elections Infrastructure Information Sharing and Analysis Center (EI-ISAC).[6] CISA is working with the vendor community as well, through the Election Infrastructure Subsector Coordinating Council.[7] Beyond CISA, the U.S. Election Assistance Commission (EAC) establishes voluntary voting system guidelines, certifies labs to test election equipment, and manages the distribution of federal funds appropriated under the Help America Vote Act (HAVA) to the states and territories.[8] These activities illustrate that the federal government takes the cybersecurity of elections seriously and is actively pursuing constructive partnerships with state and local election officials, who are primarily responsible for conducting elections in the United States. State and local election officials, meanwhile, are faced with trying to understand where cybersecurity risk lies in their systems, how they can prioritize that risk, how to focus their efforts and limited resources to address that risk, and how they can best take advantage of the services available to them from

---

[5]   CISA, "Election Infrastructure Security," last revised May 13, 2020.

[6]   Center for Internet Security, "Elections Infrastructure ISAC," undated.

[7]   CISA, "Government Facilities Sector—Election Infrastructure Subsector: Charters and Membership," last revised May 8, 2019.

[8]   EAC, "About the U.S. EAC," undated a; Public Law 107-252, Help America Vote Act of 2002, October 29, 2002.

CISA and the EI-ISAC. The methodology laid out in this report is one approach to help them with these questions.

Tackling cybersecurity creates several challenges, however, as we illustrate in this report. The first is that election systems in the United States are uniquely diverse because of the federal nature of our system of government. This includes the technology used to conduct elections, as well as the governance of election systems, which vary by state and even within states.[9] From a national perspective, this diversity presents challenges for the federal government in understanding where risk lies and how to prioritize efforts to support state and local governments. In this report, we lay out our approach to evaluating and prioritizing risk in election systems to provide election officials and other stakeholders at all levels with insights into how to prioritize efforts to address cyber risks. We start by discussing the diversity of election systems and why traditional approaches to evaluating risk are not well suited to the problem. We then lay out our approach for understanding relative risk within and across election systems and conclude with how this approach can be used by CISA, EAC, and state and local election officials to improve election systems' cybersecurity posture. The methodology presented here is based on work originally conducted in support of CISA's National Risk Management Center. Given the sensitive nature of the outputs of that analysis, however, and to reduce risk of informing malicious actors where we have determined that risk lies, we have chosen to illustrate our methodology with abstracted data. We note in the text where this occurs.

Diversity of Election Systems

The election system in the United States is, in reality, not one system but a tapestry of many different systems. Although they all encompass the same functions, system processes and infrastructure vary from state to state and often between jurisdictions—be they counties, parishes,

---

[9]   The U.S. territories also are responsible for conducting elections. For brevity, we refer to states but encompass the territories in that term.

towns, or cities—within states. The number of election jurisdictions in the United States is not fixed, because it depends on whether one is accounting for election jurisdictions for federal elections (i.e., for positions in the federal government) or for elections more broadly, which can include state and local offices, school boards, and the judiciary.[10] The National Conference of State Legislatures estimates that there are more than 10,000 election jurisdictions across the United States.[11] EAC's Election Administration and Voting Survey covers nearly 6,500 jurisdictions across the 50 U.S. states, the District of Columbia, and four U.S. territories and targets jurisdictions that are responsible for conducting elections for federal office.[12] Then–CISA director Christopher C. Krebs has spoken of 8,800 jurisdictions and entities, which accounts for overlapping responsibilities within and across some jurisdictions particularly in such states as Arizona, Minnesota, and New Jersey.[13]

States and local jurisdictions vary in terms of the technology they use to conduct elections and in terms of their governance structures. HAVA was a response to problems in the 2000 presidential election. Congress appropriated more than $1.5 billion to assist states in modernizing infrastructure and establishing minimum standards for administering elections.[14] Many states used these funds, including more-recent appropriations in 2018 and 2020, to address cybersecurity concerns by training personnel, conducting penetration testing of networks, and conducting tabletop exercises.

---

[10] For example, federal elections, such as for the U.S. House of Representatives, are organized by the county registrar in Los Angeles County, but local city elections are run by the City of Los Angeles in years when they do not coincide with federal elections.

[11] National Conference of State Legislatures, "Election Administration at State and Local Levels," February 3, 2020.

[12] EAC, *Election Administration and Voting Survey: 2018 Comprehensive Report*, Washington, D.C., 2019.

[13] Jeff Elder, "DHS Is Worried About Ransomware and Other Cybersecurity Attacks on Voter Registration Databases Ahead of the Election, Says Top Official," *Business Insider*, February 25, 2020; email exchange with National Risk Management Center analyst, March 31, 2020.

[14] EAC, "Help America Vote Act," undated b.

In the United States, elections are administered and run by state and local governments. In almost half the states, the secretary of state is the chief election official (and usually an elected official). Alaska's and Utah's chief election officials are the lieutenant governors. Hawaii, Illinois, Maryland, New York, North Carolina, Oklahoma, South Carolina, Virginia, and Wisconsin, on the other hand, have election commissions.[15] HAVA requires every state (except North Dakota) to maintain a statewide record of voter registration, but how this is administered also varies by state.[16] In so-called "top-down" states, the voter registration database (VRDB) of record is controlled at the state level, whereas, in "bottom-up" states, the VRDB of record is held by each local jurisdiction and the state maintains a copy. A few states operate a "hybrid" system in which some counties use the state-level registration system while others maintain their own. Arizona, Florida, and Texas are hybrid states, for example.[17]

The level of centralization also varies for other components of the election system, which we describe in more detail later in this report. Some states, such as Georgia and South Carolina, are more uniform in conducting ballot and electronic pollbook preparation and using the same vote-casting technology on a statewide basis, whereas other states, such as Kentucky and California, are more diverse in terms of day-of-vote infrastructure (e.g., different types of voting machines, use of networked versus nonnetworked pollbooks). Later in this report, we describe the election system.

Finally, electoral jurisdictions also vary in size, with some having as few as 100 voters and the largest encompassing several million voters.[18] For example, the largest jurisdiction in California, Los Angeles County, has 5.5 million registered voters, while one of the small-

---

[15] National Conference of State Legislatures, 2020.

[16] North Dakota is exempt from this mandate because the state allows any state resident to vote by presenting valid identification and requires no prior registration.

[17] EAC, "Statewide Voter Registration Systems," blog post, August 31, 2017.

[18] David C. Kimball and Brady Baybeck, "Are All Jurisdictions Equal? Size Disparity in Election Administration," *Election Law Journal*, Vol. 12, No. 2, June 2013, pp. 130–145.

est, Modoc County, has 5,000.[19] This diversity presents a challenge in assessing risk from a national perspective, both in terms of availability of data and for developing a method that can reasonably apply to jurisdictions large and small.

This report provides an overview of the approach that researchers at the Homeland Security Operational Analysis Center developed to prioritize risk in election systems in the United States. We start in the next chapter with a discussion of how to think about risk assessment for heterogeneous systems, then we discuss how to apply risk assessment to election systems.

---

[19] California Secretary of State, "Report of Registration—February 18, 2020: Registration by County," 2020.

CHAPTER TWO

An Approach to Prioritizing Risk

In this chapter, we examine whether and how current approaches to risk assessment and prioritization can be applied to election systems. As noted in Chapter One, U.S. election infrastructure is diverse in terms of the technology, how it is implemented, who owns and operates it, and its configuration.[1] In addition, not all election infrastructure is of the same type, although there has been a migration more recently to common platforms. Election systems are heterogeneous, both across the system components and within a given election system function, traversing technology types from analog to digital. This presents challenges from a risk assessment perspective that can be illustrated by a question that an election official might ask: "How can I compare my state-level VRDB's risk with the risk to my vote tabulation machine?" The question is no easier when asking the extent to which we can compare risk for a VRDB in a large jurisdiction, such as Harris County, Texas, with more than 2 million voters, to risk to the VRDB in Wyoming, with roughly 250,000 voters.

Comparing the risks associated with different types of attacks, on different components, in different jurisdictions, presents many challenges. There are questions about the nature of the threat and what effect different types of attacks might have on an election. There are questions of scale of attacks and how to normalize risk across jurisdictions and states. There are also questions about the vulnerabilities in

---

[1] It should be noted that many countries have much more–centrally managed and controlled national elections, which presents different challenges but certainly simplifies the assessment of risk.

these components and understanding where systemic risk might occur. In this chapter, we start by examining how risk is addressed in complex systems more generally, then follow by discussing how this presents in election systems.

The National Institute of Standards and Technology's Risk Assessment Approach

Risk assessment methods have a long history and cross multiple disciplines, from fire hazards to emergency management and health care.[2] The *DHS Risk Lexicon* defines *risk* as the "potential for an unwanted outcome resulting from an incident, event, or occurrence, as determined by its likelihood and the associated consequences."[3] The National Institute of Standards and Technology (NIST) definition is nearly identical, albeit phrased in a different order. NIST defines *risk* as

> a measure of the extent to which an entity is threatened by a potential circumstance or event, and is typically a function of: (i) the adverse impacts that would arise if the circumstance or event occurs; and (ii) the likelihood of occurrence.[4]

---

[2] Federal Emergency Management Agency, *Threat and Hazard Identification and Risk Assessment (THIRA) and Stakeholder Preparedness Review (SPR) Guide*, Washington, D.C., Comprehensive Preparedness Guide 201, 3rd ed., May 29, 2018; Ron Z. Goetzel, Paula Staley, Lydia Ogden, Paul Stange, Jared Fox, Jason Spangler, Maryam Tabrizi, Meghan Beckowski, Niranjana Kowlessar, Russell E. Glasgow, Martina V. Taylor, and Chelsea Richards, *A Framework for Patient-Centered Health Risk Assessments: Providing Health Promotion and Disease Prevention Services to Medicare Beneficiaries*, Atlanta, Ga.: U.S. Department of Health and Human Services, Centers for Disease Control and Prevention, Office of the Associate Director for Policy, 2011; National Fire Protection Association, *Guide for the Evaluation of Fire Risk Assessments*, Quincy, Mass., NFPA 551, 2019.

[3] Risk Steering Committee, DHS, *DHS Risk Lexicon*, 2010 ed., last revised May 28, 2019, p. 27.

[4] Joint Task Force Transformation Initiative, *Guide for Conducting Risk Assessments*, Gaithersburg, Md.: National Institute of Standards and Technology, U.S. Department of Commerce, Special Publication 800-30, revision 1, September 2012, p. 6.

Because the definitions are compatible, we used the NIST risk assessment approach as the starting point for our work.

NIST guidance states that a risk assessment methodology should be chosen to fit an organization's needs and its risk management strategy. In general, risk assessment should therefore use some form of risk model that accounts for such factors as threat, vulnerability, impact, and consequence.[5] NIST's risk assessment approach is divided into three tiers encompassing organizational-level (tier 1), mission-level (tier 2), and information system–level (tier 3) assessments. The level of assessment indicates the type of activities the risk assessment can influence, such as security policies at the organizational level, enterprise architecture design choices at the mission level, and selection of security controls at the information system level.[6] These levels are not mutually exclusive, and implications can cross the tiers, such as design choices or how security policies are translated into security controls (and vice versa).

The NIST risk assessment itself encompasses five steps:

1. Identify threat sources and events.
2. Identify vulnerabilities and predisposing conditions.
3. Determine the likelihood of occurrence.
4. Determine the magnitude of impact.
5. Determine risk.[7]

Our approach largely follows these steps, with some modifications, as we note in the discussion.

---

[5] Joint Task Force Transformation Initiative, 2012, p. 8.

[6] Joint Task Force Transformation Initiative, 2012, p. 17.

[7] Joint Task Force Transformation Initiative, 2012, p. 23. Although the NIST process uses five steps, ours is a three-step process.

Components of Election Infrastructure

The risk prioritization method presented in this report addresses components of the election system that are under the control or are the responsibility of state or local election officials. It is intended to provide a high-level view of relative risk across election system components. It does not address election cybersecurity risk to candidates, political campaigns, social media platforms, or other aspects of elections not under the direct control of election officials. Nor does it address risks to other critical infrastructure—such as electrical or transportation infrastructure—that might have an effect on elections. We also did not address disinformation or influence campaigns regardless of whether such efforts use digital media. It is important to note as well that the risks we assessed are direct cybersecurity risks—that is, the potential risks of a cyber attack on a component of the election system. This risk prioritization method does not *directly* measure the secondary and tertiary effects of such attacks, such as the potential for loss of public confidence in the election process, which can have a significant impact on the smooth running of elections. Those effects are indirectly accounted for as a component of risk through our severity value (for a discussion of severity, see the "Consequence" section later in this chapter). Given these caveats, the methodology covers the main components of election infrastructure in the United States and is intended to assist election officials in understanding and prioritizing risk and in taking steps to mitigate the greatest risk, where possible.

Elections are not simply about voting. Other processes must function to enable people to vote and to ensure that those votes are counted and reported. Consequently, in our analysis, we examined the following components of the election system:

- voter registration
- pollbooks
- voting machines
- tabulation
- official websites.

We focus on these components because they cover the phases of the election process and represent the components that are under the direct influence or control of election officials at the state and local levels and the vendor community that supports elections, as well as federal partners supporting cybersecurity efforts—this is the community we primarily seek to inform.

As depicted in the process map shown in Figure 2.1, each of these components has its own important role to play in the overall election system, such that a failure in any component could compromise the potential of a free and fair election. Furthermore, the role each component plays is not limited to what is seen on Election Day. There are processes that occur before the election to prepare the components for use. We describe the components in turn below.

- **Voter registration** is a nearly continuous process to create new registration records, update information in existing records, and remove outdated records.[8] A prospective voter can register in person, online, or, in some cases, by phone or mail. Our analysis encompasses the technology and processes used to enter, store,

Figure 2.1
Process Map Depicting Election System Components Considered in Our Analysis

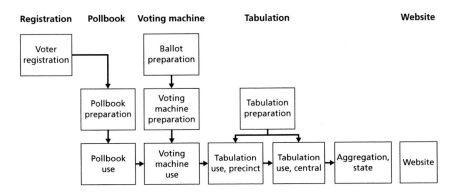

---

[8] Many states have registration deadlines in advance of elections, after which time a prospective voter is not allowed to register to vote in that election. A few states allow for same-

and edit voter registration information. This includes the servers used to host the database and web portals used for access. Voter registration databases receive data from a variety of sources, including other government agencies (e.g., departments of motor vehicles) and organizations that aid in the registration process (e.g., organizations that run voter registration campaigns). During our analysis, we did not evaluate these other systems, but we did account for information flows and connections with such sources.

- **Pollbooks** contain information on registered voters at polling locations and can be used to register voters where permitted by law. Before pollbooks can be used, they must first be prepared by transferring information from the voter registration database. Consequently, our analysis encompassed the technology and processes used to create and use (e.g., view, edit, or modify voter records) pollbooks for elections. This may include both networked and non-networked pollbooks, where non-networked pollbooks are local paper copies or static files on some form of electronic media. Networked pollbooks are electronic pollbooks with a connection to an external database, which may include direct connection to the voter registration database or a separate server or proxy.

- **Ballot preparation** is the process of laying out electoral contests and candidates and then translating those layouts into various forms, such as the file for printing paper ballots, as well as the files for audio and electronic interface and visual ballots. Additionally, it generates the files used for tabulating those ballots within the voting machine. This process is usually completed in ballot layout and ballot generation applications, typically within an election management system.

- **Voting machines** are the most visible form of technology with which voters interact in the voting process. Our analysis encompassed the technology and processes that election officials use to

---

day registration or provisional registration after the official registration cutoff date. For a state-by-state overview of registration deadlines, see Vote.org, "Voter Registration Deadlines," undated.

prepare vote-casting machines for ballot presentation and tabulation, including loading the ballot files described in "ballot preparation" above. Additionally, it encompassed the technology and processes that voters use to cast their ballots. This includes paper-based vote casting, electronic ballot-marking devices, and direct-recording electronic machines with or without a voter-verified paper audit trail.

- **Tabulation** is the means by which choices on individual ballots are counted and aggregated from summary reports to determine the result of a contest. Our analysis encompasses the technology and processes used to count votes and aggregate results. Vote tabulation may occur at the precinct level in addition to a central level. Vote tabulation processes include hand counting, optical scans of paper ballots, and direct electronic tabulation.
- State- and local-level election officials use official **websites** to communicate information to the public, including how to register to vote, where to vote (e.g., precinct lookup tool), and contest results. In some cases, election websites are hosted on government-owned infrastructure, but they are often hosted by commercial partners.

In addition to these main functions, there are other elements, such as post-election audits. We did not assess those independently because audits involving recounting physical ballots use the same technology as that used in tabulation. Risk-limiting audits are a statistically informed approach to auditing an election, sometimes supported by a software program to determine the number of ballots to review but still relying on the same types of technology (or humans) to conduct the review.[9]

As noted above, our analysis focuses on the election system components central to the conduct of elections. Elections, of course, are carried out in a broader ecosystem, encompassing political parties, interest groups, media outlets of various types, corporations, and the voting public. Cybersecurity concerns also affect these stakeholders.

---

[9] See, for example, Colorado Secretary of State, "Understanding Risk Limiting Audits," undated. Also see Mark Lindeman and Philip B. Stark, "A Gentle Introduction to Risk-Limiting Audits," *IEEE Security and Privacy: Special Issue on Electronic Voting*, Vol. 10, No. 5, September–October 2012, pp. 42–49.

Political parties use technology to track prospective voters, engage them across a variety of media platforms, and conduct their campaigns. This applies as well to interest groups and corporations that actively engage in the public debate over policies, issues, and candidates. Media outlets, whether more-traditional forms (e.g., radio, television, or print) or forms of more-recent advent (e.g., social media, such as Facebook or Twitter), also play an important role in disseminating information (or disinformation), shaping public opinion, and providing a means for candidates and campaigns to engage with the voting public. These platforms are also subject to potential cyber threats. They are, however, beyond an election official's control or influence to address potential vulnerabilities to cyber threats.

Adapting Risk Assessment for Election Systems

There are several challenges in conducting a risk assessment of election systems. Risk assessment usually involves some form of understanding the probability of an adverse action occurring (i.e., what is the likelihood of an attack occurring?) and the consequences of such an attack. First, to address the question of probability of attack, one can make assessments, but the array of potential actors is quite broad, from nation-state actors with a vested interest in interfering in another country's elections, to a lone hacktivist seeking to make a political statement, or even an individual who is fascinated by the possibilities but does not have a specific goal in mind. Finally, there may be actors with more-prosaic but nonetheless harmful motivations, such as seeking to support a compatriot's election or undermine another candidate. There is significant uncertainty surrounding the likelihood of each of these types of attackers.[10]

As noted above, the NIST approach consists of five steps:

1. Identify threat sources and events.

---

[10] This same insight arose in addressing the risk of terrorist attacks. See Henry H. Willis, Andrew R. Morral, Terrence Kelly, and Jamison Jo Medby, *Estimating Terrorism Risk*, Santa Monica, Calif.: RAND Corporation, MG-388-RC, 2005, p. 13.

2. Identify vulnerabilities and predisposing conditions.
3. Determine the likelihood of occurrence.
4. Determine the magnitude of impact.
5. Determine risk.

We essentially follow the NIST approach but, for simplicity, combine some of its steps into three main questions:

- What types of events (cyber attacks) may occur?
- What is the likelihood of a successful attack?
- Assuming that an attack is successful, what are the consequences of the attack?

Our assessment of election systems considered different types of attacks on different election system components. For each attack on each component, as we demonstrate below, we assumed that the adversary's intent to attack was a given (i.e., the probability is 1) and differentiate likelihood by analyzing the level of adversary capability required to conduct a cyber attack against an election system component. This is a departure from the standard approach for risk assessment, in which an organization attempts to assign probability to a given risk factor based on the likelihood an adversary actor will initiate an action and the probability that it will have an impact on the targeted system.[11] Indeed, assuming a probability of attack of 1 could potentially lead to an overestimation of the likelihood of attack, but, because we were interested in evaluating *relative* risk across election system components, making that assumption would not affect the prioritization results. We then examined the associated consequences of the attack, addressing both the potential scale of impact for a cyber attack on an election system component and the importance the election community places on the consequences of that attack. In the rest of this chapter, we explain the approach and rationale for each of these components of risk.

---

[11] Joint Task Force Transformation Initiative, 2012, p. 10.

Types of Attacks

An adversary might seek to compromise election infrastructure to accomplish different goals. We distinguished three types of attacks to each election infrastructure component using the CIA (confidentiality, integrity, and availability) triad commonly used in cybersecurity:[12]

- A **confidentiality attack** is aimed at the theft and unauthorized use of confidential information. The adversary might use stolen information for a variety of purposes, including for intelligence goals or for public dissemination (e.g., doxing) that causes confusion or undermines the credibility of elections. These confidentiality attacks may include the theft and dissemination of information related to voter registration records or actual votes cast. Although some components contain information that is intended to become public eventually, we have included assessment of confidentiality attacks on these components for completeness and because there may be some reasons an adversary would seek to gain access to such information. For example, a vote tabulation is intended to become public soon after the polls close, but an adversary may derive an information arbitrage advantage from learning the results of an election or referendum early, or it might seek to drive down voter participation by signaling early that a contest is a foregone conclusion. Additionally, some voter registration information is protected because it may contain such information as the home addresses of judges and law enforcement officials or full social security numbers for voters.

- An **integrity attack** is intended to alter the primary function of, or the data stored within, the targeted election system component. These attacks may include changing voter registration records, attempting to alter the outcome of an election by changing votes recorded or the tabulation of such votes, or manipulating the election results reported on official websites to spread false information.

---

[12] Shon Harris, *CISSP Exam Guide*, 6th ed., New York: McGraw Hill, 2013, pp. 22–25.

- An **availability attack** is intended primarily to disrupt and deny the normal functions of election system components but does not affect the integrity of the system. These types of attacks may take the form of denial-of-service attacks, ransomware, or any other mechanism that disrupts normal functions of specific election system components.

Attacks on the confidentiality, integrity, or availability of election system components might also have consequences for the public confidence in the credibility of the elections. The mere claim of an integrity attack on vote tabulation in a specific jurisdiction might decrease public confidence in the election outcome or prompt legal challenges. We did not directly assess attacks that seek to undermine the public confidence of the credibility of elections, candidates, or specific issues that do not involve actual attacks on the confidentiality, integrity, or availability of elections. That said, one or more of the attack types we address may have undermining public confidence as its primary or secondary objective.

Likelihood

Given the attack types, how can we understand the potential for these attacks to occur across election system components, and how do we apply a comparable approach to evaluating the consequences of such attacks? As we noted earlier, NIST prescribes an approach to risk assessments that examines the likelihood for an adversarial threat (as opposed to safety or other system malfunctions) based on evaluating adversary intent, capability, and targeting.[13] In the case of elections, detailed information on any particular threat actor's intent is limited and might not be readily available to state and local election officials.[14] Similarly, data on adversary targeting are also limited and potentially unavailable. Because of these limitations, we made a simplifying assumption: We assumed that an adversary's intent to conduct

---

[13] Joint Task Force Transformation Initiative, 2012, p. 10.

[14] Federal partners at DHS and the Federal Bureau of Investigation are expanding programs to provide clearances and threat briefings to election officials.

an attack exists and that the adversary would choose the type of attack and component to attack based on how easy it would be to attack the component and the consequence of such an attack.

In our analysis of likelihood, we instead focused on the adversary capabilities required to execute a given attack against each election component. To execute a specific attack, the adversary would have to compromise relevant election system components by exploiting vulnerability and exposure. These vulnerabilities and exposures are not all exploited the same way, and the adversary would need to pursue specific attack paths depending on the specific ways the election system is set up. Different capabilities and levels of attacker sophistication are required to successfully attack specific components. Under this logic, an attack that requires more-sophisticated capabilities would be less likely (i.e., have a lower likelihood) than an attack that is easier to execute. We used fault tree analysis as an analytical framework for assessing the adversary capabilities for each type of attack on specific election system components.

Threat Tiering

In the absence of detailed insights into an adversary's intent in attacking an election system (and not relying on historical information that might not reflect what an adversary will seek to do in the future), we focused on capabilities needed to execute a successful attack. Specifically, for the likelihood portion of risk, it is based on the lowest level of actor sophistication required to successfully attack an election system component. We have defined three general tiers of actors for this purpose:

- **Tier 1** are the most-capable threat actors that can discover new vulnerabilities (zero-days, or vulnerabilities in hardware or software not previously known and against which there is no known remedy or protection), develop custom exploits and tools, and combine online activities with close physical operations. These can include both nation-state and sophisticated subnational groups.

- **Tier 2** are moderately capable threat actors that can exploit most cyber vulnerabilities with sufficient time and can create their own custom exploits and tools. They are largely limited to conducting operations over the internet, although they can also exploit proximate access (e.g., wardriving, or cruising for unsecured wireless networks) or lax security policies on removable media.
- **Tier 3** are the least sophisticated threat actors and rely on readily available cyber tools to exploit known vulnerabilities. They do not create their own exploits or tools but can find them on the dark web or in existing tool suites.

The threat tiers are intentionally not tied directly to a specific actor type or advanced persistent threat group. The use of three tiers of threat actors as opposed to other taxonomies is also intentional, to provide a relatively simple method of differentiating likelihood and to account for the subjectivity involved in evaluating the level of sophistication required. We examined other models for describing tiers of adversary capability, including those developed by the Defense Science Board's Task Force on Resilient Military Systems (which used a six-tier taxonomy) and Sandia National Laboratories' Information Design Assurance Red Team system (which identifies eight tiers). These other approaches to describing actor sophistication would provide more differentiation in potential likelihood but introduce a level of perceived precision that is difficult to support with rigor and could change more rapidly over time.[15] In the next section, we describe how to apply the threat tiers.

Fault Tree Analysis

In our risk prioritization, we used fault tree analysis to identify ways in which an actor could take advantage of an election component's

---

[15] For more on the Defense Science Board, see Defense Science Board, *Task Force Report: Resilient Military Systems and the Advanced Cyber Threat*, Washington, D.C., January 2013, pp. 21–25. For more on the Sandia approach, see David P. Duggan, Sherry R. Thomas, Cynthia K. K. Veitch, and Laura Woodard, *Categorizing Threat: Building and Using a Generic Threat Matrix*, Albuquerque, N.M.: Sandia National Laboratory, SAND2007-5791, September 2007.

vulnerabilities and identify exposures to compromise that component. For each election system component, the fault trees present what actions and pathways an adversary must take to successfully execute the attack. The adversary sophistication required to conduct a specified attack on an election system component depends on how the system is set up (e.g., access modes, security controls) and thus the system's exposure. The fault trees identify which security controls or infrastructure implementations would differentiate the level of sophistication required. The fault trees, therefore, do not identify every possible configuration, vulnerability, or exposure. As a check on our approach, we compared our fault trees to the MITRE Adversarial Tactics, Techniques, and Common Knowledge (ATT&CK) framework—a widely used framework for mapping cyber attack pathways—to ensure that we had accounted for pathways an adversary might seek to use to execute an attack, such as initial access through spear-phishing or removable media.[16] The fault trees facilitate identifying how easy or difficult it would be for an adversary to execute an attack against an election system component depending on how the system component is set up. This also facilitates identifying actions to make it harder for adversaries to successfully attack a component.

This approach is intended to provide a straightforward method for distinguishing between actor capability levels by focusing on classes of exposure an adversary could exploit rather than specific technical vulnerabilities. Additionally, the fault trees can be used to develop a limited set of questions to address in characterizing and evaluating risk in election systems.

We used our tiering approach in conjunction with fault tree analysis of each attack type on each election system component. Each component was examined both in terms of preparation of systems for those that are not in constant use (i.e., pollbooks, voting machines, tabulation machines) to account for systems that are potentially epi-

---

[16] MITRE ATT&CK, homepage, undated. Note that ATT&CK was originally developed to document common techniques used by malicious cyber actors against Windows-based networks, but, at the higher levels, the tactics and techniques apply regardless of operating system.

sodically networked but not at all times and for when the system component is in use.

To demonstrate the fault tree approach, we show one of the fault trees for an integrity attack on a VRDB in Figure 2.2. We present one fault tree here, but the same analysis can be applied to each of the system components.

The adversary's objective is shown in the box at the far left of the figure—to change voter registration information. To accomplish this, an adversary has to either gain privileged access to the data itself ("data at rest") or during transmission ("data in motion"). This choice is represented as an *or* statement. Intercepting data during transit requires executing a man-in-the-middle (MITM) attack, usually through compromising the infrastructure across which the data transit. Compromising this infrastructure (such as attacking a router on the backbone infrastructure) is difficult to achieve and therefore is assessed as an attack requiring the sophistication of a tier 1 (most capable) actor. On the other hand, an adversary may seek to attack a VRDB on a state or jurisdiction's internal networks. Doing this requires both access to the database and having privileges to change information in the database (denoted by the *and* operator in the figure). It is not sufficient to be able to read the information in the database.

Accessing the database can occur through either proximate access (i.e., wireless), remote access, or physical access (which could include compromising the database through use of an unwitting legitimate user with an infected universal serial bus [USB] drive, or thumb drive). The adversary can seek to exploit any of these pathways (if they are available) but needs to use only one to succeed. The subsequent pathways marked by *if* boxes are exclusive questions. For example, for exploiting user credentials, the fault tree presents a choice on user authentication between either a username and password and use of some form of multifactor authentication (MFA) (e.g., a token or code). Our analysis focused not on identifying every potential vulnerability in a system but on identifying security controls and infrastructure implementations that lead to differentiation in the level of actor sophistication required to exploit vulnerabilities or exposures to successfully attack the system. For example, if the VRDB is accessible remotely and an intrusion pre-

Figure 2.2
Voter Registration Database: Integrity Attack

Integrity attack: Change voter registration information.

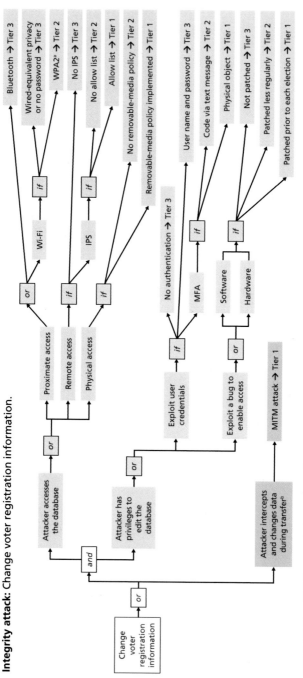

NOTE: WPAx = Wi-Fi protected access x, where x indicates the version.
[a] For our purposes, WPA is similar to wired-equivalent privacy, given advances in adversary techniques. WPA3 is not yet widely used.
[b] If data are not transferred in the maintenance process, the MITM branch does not apply.

vention system (IPS) is implemented in combination with an allow list (i.e., only certain internet protocol addresses are allowable traffic), then the actor sophistication required is assessed as tier 1. On the other hand, no IPS would make it accessible by a tier 3 actor.

A confidentiality attack would have similar characteristics to those of an integrity attack because it requires the attacker to execute similar actions to gain access to and exfiltrate data. An availability attack, on the other hand, would not require privileged access to the system, because the purpose of this type of attack is to deny the use of the system to legitimate users. Similar fault trees can be used to evaluate other components of the election system. The responses to the questions may vary depending on the security controls in place and how the system is used.

To obtain the likelihood rating for the particular type of attack on the component in question—an integrity attack on the voter registration system in our example here—a reader would first walk through each path and, based on the answer to the *if* questions corresponding to how their system is configured, determine the rating for that path. Some paths might be tier 1 while other paths are tier 3.

The reader would then resolve the *or* and *and* statements. For two or more paths connected by an *or*, an attack can be carried out by any one of the paths. In such cases, an attacker could choose the easiest path, so the rating would be the lowest tier among them: If an attack can be carried out by one tier 1 path *or* another path that is tier 3, that branch is assessed as a tier 3. For two or more paths connected by an *and*, all paths must be executed for an attack to succeed. In such cases, the hardest path must be among those executed by the attacker, so the rating would be the highest tier among them: If the attack branch requires a tier 1 path *and* a tier 3 path, then that branch is assessed as a tier 1.

Our approach to assigning a tier of actor (tier 1, 2, or 3) started from our collective knowledge and experience in evaluating cybersecurity risk, supplemented with research on the current understanding of relative sophistication required to execute attacks. For example, we assessed that exploiting unpatched software vulnerabilities is attainable for a tier 3 unsophisticated actor because there are readily available tools to assist in identifying and exploiting those vulnerabilities (e.g., the Metasploit tool suite). Exploiting user credentials where MFA is employed is more difficult and would require an actor with greater sophistication, particularly if the form of authentication includes a physical token, as opposed to a code sent by text message, which has already been subject to exploitation.[17] These assessments of actor sophistication are likely to change over time, however, so they will require periodic reevaluation. For example, WPA2 is currently the most widely employed form of Wi-Fi encryption, but the emergence of WPA3 and the likelihood that cyber actors will develop ways to exploit WPA2 are likely to lower the level of sophistication required to break that encryption. Creating fault trees for the remaining components and attack types follows the same approach. For election officials and others supporting this analysis, personnel should have expertise in cybersecurity and adversary tactics, techniques, and procedures.

The fault trees can be used to derive actor capability levels and then inform risk prioritization. This approach can be used at the state or local level to develop a view of the likelihood of the different attack types on each election system component.

Consequence

The other element of risk is consequence. In other contexts, the consequence of an attack may be expressed in terms of the dollar value of damage incurred or lives lost. In the context of election cybersecurity, assessing consequences is not quite as straightforward. First, assessing the number of voters affected by an attack is difficult because election systems differ by jurisdiction and jurisdictions vary in size. Consequently, it is not possible to give a single estimate of the number of people affected by an attack, even if the attack could be said to affect the entire jurisdiction. Providing a range of numbers of potentially affected voters would also provide limited insight because many of the ranges could be quite broad (from one voter to several million in some cases) and therefore not illuminating of relative risk.

---

[17] Matt Elliott, "Do You Use SMS for Two-Factor Authentication? Here's Why You Shouldn't," *CNET*, April 8, 2020.

Second, different types of attacks on different election system components produce very different kinds of impacts. To an extent, the type of attack and the component attacked defines the impact: An availability attack on pollbooks has the consequence that pollbooks cannot be used on Election Day, which interferes with people's ability to vote; an integrity attack on voting machines changes the record of votes. However, it is not readily apparent how one should prioritize across such different impacts. Election officials may place different weight on how important those impacts are.

Although assessing consequences precisely is difficult, for the purposes of prioritizing risks, we estimated it in terms of two elements, **scale** and **severity**. The first element, the **scale** of impact of an attack, is a measure of how widespread the direct effects would be, given a successful attack on a particular component of the election system. An attack on a particular component could affect just that machine, or it could affect the entire jurisdiction, or it could affect multiple jurisdictions. Because jurisdictions differ in size, we are unable to be any more quantitative about the number of people who are affected. However, all else being equal, an attack that affects an entire jurisdiction affects more people than one that affects just one machine, and thus would be considered higher consequence. An attack that affects multiple jurisdictions affects even more people yet. Thus, we used scale as a proxy for the number of people who would be affected by an attack and assessed it based on how an election system is set up and where the attacked component fits within that system.

The second element in our estimate of consequence is the relative **severity** of the attack. We use the severity rating as a way to prioritize different types of attacks on different types of components: If all else (i.e., likelihood, scale) were equal, how much would different types of attacks affect a jurisdiction's ability to conduct its election? The severity rating thus represents the relative weight that the election community places on different attacks. The ratings are the product of an expert elicitation process. It represents experts' judgment on the impact of, for instance, an availability attack on an election-night reporting website, relative to a confidentiality attack on the VRDB. Some attacks might be highly likely and have the potential to directly affect a large number of people yet be deemed by election officials to be of relatively low severity. A reason for this could be that election officials can readily recover from them. For example, an availability attack on ballot preparation could hamper the election for an entire jurisdiction, but, all things considered, might be considered relatively low severity in that such an attack would be discovered in advance of Election Day and officials could ensure that they have options for repairing the problem. On the other hand, some attacks might be very difficult to conduct at scale, but even a small-scale attack would be considered relatively severe, because of the effect the attack would have on the outcome of an election or on people's perceptions of the legitimacy of the results.

Together, the measures of scale and severity make up our estimate of the consequences of different types of attacks on different components of the election system. In the rest of this section, we go into more detail on how we estimated the measures of scale and severity.

Scale

The scale of a cyber attack's effects is a measure of how widespread or extensive its effects could be, given one operation against a single component. We assessed scale based on the type of attack, the specific election component attacked, and how that component is integrated into the jurisdiction's election infrastructure.[18]

We categorized the scale of an attack into one of three categories:

- **low:** affecting a single machine or location
- **medium:** affecting an entire jurisdiction
- **high:** affecting an entire state or multiple jurisdictions.

In election systems, some components will be potentially vulnerable to an adversary's attack in different ways depending on the phase of an election or the way election officials are interacting with the components. Some considerations are whether the component is being prepared for subsequent use or being used, whether component technol-

---

[18] Note that we did not assess scale based on the size of population of a state or jurisdiction. States and jurisdictions vary considerably in population. More on circumstances in which such distinctions might be used are discussed at the end of this section.

ogy is networked to facilitate preparation or use, and the degree to which components are centralized or distributed. These are not mutually exclusive considerations.

- **Preparation of machines.** All else being equal, the scale of an attack will be more widespread if it happens during the preparation or programming of election machines, as opposed to during machine use. For instance, an integrity attack on a single voting machine in a precinct affects that machine or precinct, but attacks on a jurisdiction's central preparation or programming of machines could affect the entire jurisdiction using the attacked component. If machines are prepared at the state level, attacks on the preparation process could affect the entire state.
- **Networking.** All else being equal, the scale of an attack will be more widespread if it compromises networked election infrastructure. For instance, in some jurisdictions, e-pollbooks are networked together across the jurisdiction to facilitate the operation of voting centers, whereas an attack on an individual non-networked pollbook will not spread to infect others as long as it remains isolated from a network. An integrity attack on a networked e-pollbook could affect an entire jurisdiction, while an integrity attack on a local, non-networked pollbook would affect only that particular voting location.
- **Centralization.** All else being equal, the scale of an attack will be larger if it is against a centralized database or process than if it is against a localized database or process. For instance, some states are characterized as "top-down," whereby VRDBs are managed at the state level, while other states are "bottom-up," having VRDBs managed at the local level.[19] (It should be noted that, in some bottom-up systems, one jurisdiction can change records from another jurisdiction; for our purposes, we would consider that equivalent to a top-down system in terms of scale.) An integrity attack on a VRDB in a top-down state could affect an entire state, while an integrity attack on a VRDB in a bottom-up state

---

[19] EAC, 2017.

would affect only a single jurisdiction. Similarly, some jurisdictions tabulate votes at each polling location before aggregating results at a central location, while others tabulate votes only at a central location. An integrity attack on a central tabulation system or process would have a larger scale than an integrity attack on a local tabulation process.

The approach described above is best used when examining many jurisdictions and states as CISA needed for a national view of risk. Individual state and local jurisdictions may want to use an approach that is more customized to their context. One approach could include defining scale depending on whether the cyber attack would affect one location (low scale), a jurisdiction (medium scale), or a state as a whole (high scale), as we note above. However, many states have jurisdictions of very different sizes and thus may wish to differentiate between attacks on smaller jurisdictions and those on larger jurisdictions. States may also want to make the determination that an attack affecting more than one jurisdiction, even if not statewide, would nonetheless be considered large scale.

Severity

In addition to scale, we analyzed the severity of a successful attack on an election system component. Severity is an assessment of the extent to which election processes would be impeded by an attack, using expert elicitation from the election community to derive the score. The reason severity is an important element to address is that the impact ratings we derived give only a rough sense of the upper bound of immediate impact to the system itself from a successful attack. It does not tell us anything about the potential secondary effects that such attacks could have on public confidence, the resilience of the election system and processes, or the smooth running of an election, all of which are important to election officials to understand and account for in their evaluation of risk. The immediate impact of an attack is important, but its severity could mean the difference between an election being perceived as legitimate or not.

Evaluating severity is inherently subjective and can vary across election jurisdictions. All election officials have contingency plans in place to handle such situations as a voting machine breaking down or a polling center losing electrical power. Opinions and experience vary, however, on the extent to which a cyber attack on an election system component is recoverable and would affect perceptions of electoral legitimacy.

One way to address this challenge is to engage in expert elicitation to develop severity scores. In the original analysis in support of CISA, Homeland Security Operational Analysis Center researchers used expert elicitation facilitated through the Election Infrastructure Government Coordinating Council and Election Infrastructure Sector Coordinating Council to gather election officials and experts from the vendor community.[20] Expert elicitation is used here to develop severity

---

[20] The expert elicitation method is related to the RAND/UCLA appropriateness method developed in the mid-1980s by the RAND Corporation and the University of California, Los Angeles (UCLA) School of Medicine. Although this method aims to quantify the extent of agreement and disagreement among experts, the expert elicitation method aims to reach an overall consensus. The method includes the following steps: prepare, rate, provide feedback, discuss (in which items can be changed, deleted, or added), and rerate. This process is also grounded in the literature of the Delphi method, developed at the RAND Corporation in the 1950s. Delphi is a method used to conduct expert elicitation. It is structured around the assumption that, by virtue of asking the same questions in an iterative process, experts will move closer to consensus. See Siddhartha Dalal, Dmitry Khodyakov, Ramesh Srinivasan, Susan Straus, and John Adams, "ExpertLens: A System for Eliciting Opinions from a Large Pool of Non-Collocated Experts with Diverse Knowledge," *Technological Forecasting and Social Change*, Vol. 78, No. 8, October 2011, pp. 1427–1428; Kathryn Fitch, Steven J. Bernstein, Maria Dolores Aguilar, Bernard Burnand, Juan Ramon LaCalle, Pablo Lazaro, Mirjam van het Loo, Joseph McDonnell, Janneke Vader, and James P. Kahan, *The RAND/UCLA Appropriateness Method User's Manual*, Santa Monica, Calif.: RAND Corporation, MR-1269-DG-XII/RE, 2001, pp. 6–7; and Shakila Thangaratinam and Charles W. E. Redman, "The Delphi Technique," *Obstetrician and Gynaecologist*, Vol. 7, No. 2, April 2005, pp. 120–125. Also informed by discussion with RAND experts, March 26–28, 2019. For an example of an application of a structured expert panel process, refer to Sandra H. Berry, Laura M. Bogart, Chau Pham, Karin Liu, Leroy Nyberg, Michael Stoto, Marika Suttorp, and J. Quentin Clemens, "Development, Validation and Testing of an Epidemiological Case Definition of Interstitial Cystitis/Painful Bladder Syndrome," *Journal of Urology*, Vol. 183, No. 5, May 2010, pp. 1848–1852.

There are limitations and challenges associated with using expert elicitation, particularly when used to derive probabilities or to elicit a large number of technical judgments. See

scores after first discussing the cybersecurity risks to each component and the plans and processes in place to address contingencies. Discussion with experts supports gaining insights on the potentially broader effects of a successful cyber attack, such as the impact on public confidence, the perceived legitimacy of the election process, or election officials' ability to recover from and mitigate the effects of the attack. The experts were then asked to score their views on the severity of each attack type on each of the election system components on a five-point scale from 1 (little significance) to 5 (extremely significant). The experts were asked to exclude attack scale and likelihood of attack from their considerations when scoring the severity of an attack.

For the purpose of illustrating our method, notional results for an experts' group are shown in Table 2.1, with how many of the experts selected a given score for component–attack type pairing and the average of the responses. We provide notional scores given the sensitive nature of the actual outputs from the original expert group, which was used to inform CISA analysis and prioritization. The same principles for expert elicitation hold for our notional example here. The results are for a posited group of 20 experts. Ideally, the expert groups should consist of representatives from a cross-section of state and local election officials, as well as other experts, such as the vendor community, which brings an understanding of the implementation of election infrastructure. It could also include former election officials, academics specializing in elections, and election observers. In executing an expert elicitation process, we determined that it was best to encourage open discussion and exchange of experiences but not seek a group consensus on a score for each attack type-component pairing. The reason for not

---

Ralph L. Keeney and Detlof von Winterfeldt, "Eliciting Probabilities from Experts in Complex Technical Problems," *IEEE Transactions on Engineering Management*, Vol. 38, No. 3, August 1991, pp. 191–201. Additionally, expert elicitation activities need to account for and train the experts on things like qualitative measures (e.g., "more likely") to ensure that each expert is using the same language. Furthermore, elicitation has to account for cognitive biases, such as anchoring and adjustment (making judgments that are influenced by initial propositions) and availability (e.g., assessing frequency based on how easily similar events come to mind). See M. Granger Morgan, "Use (and Abuse) of Expert Elicitation in Support of Decision Making for Public Policy," *Proceedings of the National Academy of Sciences*, Vol. 111, No. 20, May 20, 2014, pp. 7176–7184.

Table 2.1
Notional Example of an Expert Group Severity Scoring

Component	Attack Type	Severity Score					Average
		1	2	3	4	5	
VRDB	Confidentiality	1	2	11	3	3	3.25
	Integrity	0	0	3	4	13	4.5
	Availability	0	0	12	5	3	3.55
Pollbook	Confidentiality	2	10	4	3	1	2.55
	Integrity	0	0	8	9	4	3.75
	Availability	2	3	10	4	1	2.95
Voting machine	Confidentiality	1	6	7	4	2	3
	Integrity	0	0	0	3	17	4.85
	Availability	2	3	4	7	4	3.4
Tabulation	Confidentiality	5	9	5	0	1	2.15
	Integrity	0	0	0	2	18	4.9
	Availability	0	5	12	1	2	3
Website	Confidentiality	9	11	0	0	0	1.55
	Integrity	0	0	3	7	10	4.35
	Availability	5	11	3	0	1	2.05

NOTE: 1 is least severe and 5 is the most severe. Each cell indicates the number of experts assigning that score to that attack type on that component.

seeking consensus on the scores is that the election experts' perspectives were informed by their experiences and knowledge of the variation in infrastructure implementations, election law and policies in different states and jurisdictions, and available mitigation options. A consensus view that settled on one score would likely not be a fair representation of these considerations.

Calculating the Risk Score

To provide a risk score, we calculated the product of the numeric representations of capability (likelihood), scale of attack, and severity. Although this product provides a single numeric value for risk, there is no standard interpretation for this value on its own. In other words, a risk "score" of 32, for example, should not be interpreted as having a specific value or importance except in terms of allowing us to differentiate relative risk. The calculation is converted for display purposes into relative tiering. As a result, this final risk score for each component–attack type is presented based on its magnitude relative to the scores of other pairs. Because the capability scores range from 1 to 3, the scale scores range from 1 to 3, and severity scores range from 1 to 5, the values of the risk score can range from a minimum possible score of 1 to a maximum possible score of 45.[21] To provide a visual representation for the purposes of prioritizing risk, in Table 2.2, we have evenly divided the possible risk scores into three color-coded categories.[22]

Table 2.2 shows notional output from the use of our methodology. The ratings for likelihood represent the ratings for a notional jurisdiction that would depend on how its components are configured, as illustrated in the fault tree in Figure 2.2. The ratings for scale depend on the networking and centralization of the notional jurisdiction's sys-

---

[21] We examined whether having importance scores range from 1 to 5 would give the importance score undue weight as compared to the other two scores, which each range from 1 to 3. However, because the risk score is computed by multiplying the three scores, whether severity scores range from 1 to 5 or are rescaled to range from 1 to 3 would not affect the relative ranking of the risks. Therefore, for the purpose of this risk prioritization, we have kept the severity ratings on the 1-to-5 scale used in the expert elicitation process. Providing a broader range for expert elicitation (1 to 5) works better with groups because it allows them to articulate gradations, rather than force them into a three-point system. We acknowledge that there is robust debate on the usefulness of different point scales. For two views on this topic, see Jacob Jacoby and Michael S. Matell, "Three-Point Likert Scales Are Good Enough," *Journal of Marketing Research*, Vol. 8, No. 4, November 1971, pp. 495–500, and Shing-On Leung, "A Comparison of Psychometric Properties and Normality in 4-, 5-, 6-, and 11-Point Likert Scales," *Journal of Social Service Research*, Vol. 37, No. 4, 2011, pp. 412–421.

[22] Note that there can be cases at the boundaries in which only one point separates a risk that falls into a dark red category from one that falls into the orange category. This can occur with any method that turns a set of scores into a smaller number of categories using fixed cutoff points.

Table 2.2
Notional Risk Prioritization Output Table

Component	Attack Type	Tier	Consequence		Risk Score	Risk Rank
			Scale	Severity		
VRDB	Confidentiality	2	High	3.25	19.5	2
	Integrity	1		4.5	13.5	5
	Availability	1		3.55	10.65	7
Pollbook	Confidentiality	2	Medium	2.55	10.2	8
	Integrity	1		3.75	7.5	12
	Availability	1		2.95	5.9	15
Voting machine	Confidentiality	2	Medium	3	12	6
	Integrity	1		4.85	9.7	10
	Availability	1		3.4	6.8	13
Tabulation	Confidentiality	2	Medium	2.15	8.6	11
	Integrity	1		4.9	9.8	9
	Availability	1		3	6	14
Website	Confidentiality	3	High	1.55	13.95	4
	Integrity	3		4.35	39.15	1
	Availability	3		2.05	18.45	3

NOTE: Tier corresponds to capability. Severity is measured on a scale of 1 (low) to 5 (extreme). Risk score is a factor of capability (tier), scale, and severity. A calculated risk score from 1 to 15 is represented using a yellow fill, from 16 to 30 with an orange fill, and 31 to 45 in dark red. The component–attack types resulting in a dark red risk score are ones that scored in the top third of possible risk scores, and can be viewed as the highest risk where higher priority should be given, while yellow areas are ones that scored in the bottom third of possible risk scores, and can be viewed as lower priority. Risk rank is from 1 to n, where n is the number of risks assessed.

tems, as well as the way in which its machines are programmed or prepared for Election Day use. The ratings for severity depend on the weight as assessed by officials in the notional jurisdiction. The risk score is calculated as the product of likelihood, scale, and importance, then binned into the three levels of risk. We deliberately chose to bin risk as red, orange, and yellow because we wanted to emphasize that risk is present regardless of ranking (typical red-yellow-green stoplight charts might give the false impression that a green category was risk-free). The numerical output of the calculation is used to provide a rank order of the risks essentially to serve as a tiebreaker between risks of the same color. For example, if two components are ranked as red and a jurisdiction does not have the resources to address both right away, the ordinal ranking can help prioritize officials' efforts.

Examining Table 2.2 can provide several useful insights for an election official. The first is that only one attack–component pairing, an integrity attack on the website, is evaluated as falling in the highest risk category (denoted by the red color and a risk score of 39.15). This reflects a high severity score, a large scale (which indicates that this might be a statewide website), and a capability rating of tier 3, which indicates that it is highly susceptible to manipulation by even the least sophisticated attacker. The second insight is that two component–attack type pairs fall into the middle category of risk—a confidentiality attack on the VRDB and an availability attack on the website. Because the website was already ranked higher for the integrity attack evaluation, an election official would already have likely used this to prioritize addressing the cybersecurity risks in that component. Therefore, the VRDB would be second. Finally, most of the component–attack type pairs fall into the lowest category of risk, as denoted by the yellow fill. This is where the risk ranking is helpful in prioritizing effort. In this illustration, voting machines might be next in order of attention ahead of pollbooks and tabulation machines because it ranks next highest (sixth for the confidentiality attack). The risk rankings are presented as a decision aid and are not intended to be rigidly applied. The election official may decide to prioritize tabulation next because of other considerations, such as timing or effort required (e.g., securing a handful of tabulation machines may take less time than securing hundreds of voting machines).

CHAPTER THREE

Applying the Risk Prioritization in Context

The approach to evaluating risk in election systems we have laid out in this report is intended to provide a first step in risk assessment but is not intended to replace more-detailed analysis and assessments, such as identifying potential vulnerabilities or misconfigurations in the specific technology an election official oversees. The risk prioritization can not only point to where risk lies but also highlight areas in which election officials can seek assistance from their vendors, CISA, the EI-ISAC, or other stakeholders.

The risk prioritization is not the end of the story. Risk prioritization is a continuous process and should be undertaken at regular intervals—at a minimum, when changes, such as acquiring new equipment or updating policies around network or component access, are implemented in the system. The risk prioritization provides a high-level view of risk but should not be taken as a substitute for more-detailed analysis of specific components that "score" as high risk.

References

Berry, Sandra H., Laura M. Bogart, Chau Pham, Karin Liu, Leroy Nyberg, Michael Stoto, Marika Suttorp, and J. Quentin Clemens, "Development, Validation and Testing of an Epidemiological Case Definition of Interstitial Cystitis/Painful Bladder Syndrome," *Journal of Urology*, Vol. 183, No. 5, May 2010, pp. 1848–1852.

California Secretary of State, "Report of Registration—February 18, 2020: Registration by County," 2020. As of July 10, 2020:
https://www.sos.ca.gov/elections/report-registration/15day-presprim-20/

Center for Internet Security, "Elections Infrastructure ISAC," undated. As of July 10, 2020:
https://www.cisecurity.org/ei-isac/

CISA—*See* Cybersecurity and Infrastructure Security Agency.

Colorado Secretary of State, "Understanding Risk Limiting Audits," undated. As of May 29, 2020:
https://www.sos.state.co.us/pubs/elections/VotingSystems/riskAuditFiles/UnderstandingRiskLimitingAudits.pdf

Cybersecurity and Infrastructure Security Agency, "Government Facilities Sector—Election Infrastructure Subsector: Charters and Membership," last revised May 8, 2019. As of July 10, 2020:
https://www.cisa.gov/government-facilities-election-infrastructure-charters-and-membership

———, "Election Infrastructure Security," last revised May 13, 2020. As of July 10, 2020:
https://www.cisa.gov/election-security

Dalal, Siddhartha, Dmitry Khodyakov, Ramesh Srinivasan, Susan Straus, and John Adams, "ExpertLens: A System for Eliciting Opinions from a Large Pool of Non-Collocated Experts with Diverse Knowledge," *Technological Forecasting and Social Change*, Vol. 78, No. 8, October 2011, pp. 1427–1428.

Defense Science Board, *Task Force Report: Resilient Military Systems and the Advanced Cyber Threat*, Washington, D.C., January 2013. As of July 9, 2020: https://dsb.cto.mil/reports/2010s/ResilientMilitarySystemsCyberThreat.pdf

Duggan, David P., Sherry R. Thomas, Cynthia K. K. Veitch, and Laura Woodard, *Categorizing Threat: Building and Using a Generic Threat Matrix*, Albuquerque, N.M.: Sandia National Laboratory, SAND2007-5791, September 2007. As of May 26, 2019:
https://idart.sandia.gov/_assets/documents/
SAND2007-5791_Categorizing-Threat_Generic-Threat-Matrix.pdf

EAC—*See* U.S. Election Assistance Commission.

Elder, Jeff, "DHS Is Worried About Ransomware and Other Cybersecurity Attacks on Voter Registration Databases Ahead of the Election, Says Top Official," *Business Insider*, February 25, 2020. As of May 29, 2020:
https://www.businessinsider.com/department-homeland-security-voter-registration-databases-security-concern-2020-2

Elliott, Matt, "Do You Use SMS for Two-Factor Authentication? Here's Why You Shouldn't," *CNET*, April 8, 2020. As of July 10, 2020:
https://www.cnet.com/how-to/
do-you-use-sms-for-two-factor-authentication-heres-why-you-shouldnt/

Federal Emergency Management Agency, *Threat and Hazard Identification and Risk Assessment (THIRA) and Stakeholder Preparedness Review (SPR) Guide*, Washington, D.C., Comprehensive Preparedness Guide 201, 3rd ed., May 29, 2018. As of July 9, 2020:
https://www.fema.gov/media-library/assets/documents/165308

FireEye, *Cyber Threat Activity Targeting Elections*, Milpitas, Calif., 2019. As of June 4, 2020:
https://www.fireeye.com/content/dam/fireeye-www/products/pdfs/pf/gov/
eb-cyber-threat-activity.pdf

Fitch, Kathryn, Steven J. Bernstein, Maria Dolores Aguilar, Bernard Burnand, Juan Ramon LaCalle, Pablo Lazaro, Mirjam van het Loo, Joseph McDonnell, Janneke Vader, and James P. Kahan, *The RAND/UCLA Appropriateness Method User's Manual*, Santa Monica, Calif.: RAND Corporation, MR-1269-DG-XII/RE, 2001. As of July 9, 2020:
https://www.rand.org/pubs/monograph_reports/MR1269.html

Goetzel, Ron Z., Paula Staley, Lydia Ogden, Paul Stange, Jared Fox, Jason Spangler, Maryam Tabrizi, Meghan Beckowski, Niranjana Kowlessar, Russell E. Glasgow, Martina V. Taylor, and Chelsea Richards, *A Framework for Patient-Centered Health Risk Assessments: Providing Health Promotion and Disease Prevention Services to Medicare Beneficiaries*, Atlanta, Ga.: U.S. Department of Health and Human Services, Centers for Disease Control and Prevention, Office of the Associate Director for Policy, 2011. As of July 9, 2020:
https://www.cdc.gov/policy/hst/hra/

Harris, Shon, *CISSP Exam Guide*, 6th ed., New York: McGraw Hill, 2013.

Jacoby, Jacob, and Michael S. Matell, "Three-Point Likert Scales Are Good Enough," *Journal of Marketing Research*, Vol. 8, No. 4, November 1971, pp. 495–500.

Joint Task Force Transformation Initiative, *Guide for Conducting Risk Assessments*, Gaithersburg, Md.: National Institute of Standards and Technology, U.S. Department of Commerce, Special Publication 800-30, revision 1, September 2012. As of July 10, 2020:
https://csrc.nist.gov/publications/detail/sp/800-30/rev-1/final

Keeney, Ralph L., and Detlof von Winterfeldt, "Eliciting Probabilities from Experts in Complex Technical Problems," *IEEE Transactions on Engineering Management*, Vol. 38, No. 3, August 1991, pp. 191–201.

Kimball, David C., and Brady Baybeck, "Are All Jurisdictions Equal? Size Disparity in Election Administration," *Election Law Journal*, Vol. 12, No. 2, June 2013, pp. 130–145.

Leung, Shing-On, "A Comparison of Psychometric Properties and Normality in 4-, 5-, 6-, and 11-Point Likert Scales," *Journal of Social Service Research*, Vol. 37, No. 4, 2011, pp. 412–421.

Lindeman, Mark, and Philip B. Stark, "A Gentle Introduction to Risk-Limiting Audits," *IEEE Security and Privacy: Special Issue on Electronic Voting*, Vol. 10, No. 5, September–October 2012, pp. 42–49.

MITRE Adversarial Tactics, Techniques, and Common Knowledge, homepage, undated. As of May 29, 2019:
https://attack.mitre.org

MITRE ATT&CK—*See* MITRE Adversary Tactics, Techniques, and Common Knowledge.

Morgan, M. Granger, "Use (and Abuse) of Expert Elicitation in Support of Decision Making for Public Policy," *Proceedings of the National Academy of Sciences*, Vol. 111, No. 20, May 20, 2014, pp. 7176–7184.

National Conference of State Legislatures, "Election Administration at State and Local Levels," February 3, 2020. As of May 26, 2019:
http://www.ncsl.org/research/elections-and-campaigns/
election-administration-at-state-and-local-levels.aspx

National Fire Protection Association, *Guide for the Evaluation of Fire Risk Assessments*, Quincy, Mass., NFPA 551, 2019.

Office of the Director of National Intelligence, National Intelligence Council, *Assessing Russian Activities and Intentions in Recent US Elections*, Intelligence Community Assessment 2017-01D, January 6, 2017. As of January 21, 2020:
https://www.dni.gov/files/documents/ICA_2017_01.pdf

Public Law 107-252, Help America Vote Act of 2002, October 29, 2002. As of July 10, 2020:
https://www.govinfo.gov/app/details/PLAW-107publ252

Public Law 107-296, Homeland Security Act of 2002, November 25, 2002. As of May 12, 2019:
https://www.govinfo.gov/app/details/PLAW-107publ296

Risk Steering Committee, U.S. Department of Homeland Security, *DHS Risk Lexicon*, 2010 ed., last revised May 28, 2019. As of April 25, 2019:
https://www.cisa.gov/dhs-risk-lexicon

Thangaratinam, Shakila, and Charles W. E. Redman, "The Delphi Technique," *Obstetrician and Gynaecologist*, Vol. 7, No. 2, April 2005, pp. 120–125.

U.S. Code, Title 6, Domestic Security; Chapter 1, Homeland Security Organization; Subchapter III, Science and Technology in Support of Homeland Security; Section 185, Federally Funded Research and Development Centers. As of May 12, 2019:
https://www.govinfo.gov/app/details/USCODE-2017-title6/
USCODE-2017-title6-chap1-subchapIII-sec185

U.S. Department of Homeland Security, Office of the Director of National Intelligence, and Federal Bureau of Investigation, "Joint DHS, ODNI, FBI Statement on Russian Malicious Cyber Activity," December 29, 2016. As of January 21, 2020:
https://www.dni.gov/index.php/ctiic-who-we-are/leadership/
308-about/organization/information-sharing-environment/
news/2108-joint-dhs-odni-fbi-statement-on-russian-malicious-cyber-activity

U.S. Election Assistance Commission, "About the U.S. EAC," undated a. As of July 10, 2020:
https://www.eac.gov/about-the-useac

———, "Help America Vote Act," undated b. As of July 10, 2020:
https://www.eac.gov/about_the_eac/help_america_vote_act.aspx

———, "Statewide Voter Registration Systems," blog post, August 31, 2017. As of July 10, 2020:
https://www.eac.gov/statewide-voter-registration-systems

———, *Election Administration and Voting Survey: 2018 Comprehensive Report*, Washington, D.C., 2019. As of July 10, 2020:
https://www.eac.gov/research-and-data/studies-and-reports

Vote.org, "Voter Registration Deadlines," undated. As of July 10, 2020:
https://www.vote.org/voter-registration-deadlines/

Willis, Henry H., Andrew R. Morral, Terrence Kelly, and Jamison Jo Medby, *Estimating Terrorism Risk*, Santa Monica, Calif.: RAND Corporation, MG-388-RC, 2005. As of July 10, 2020:
https://www.rand.org/pubs/monographs/MG388.html

Zetter, Kim, "How Close Did Russia Really Come to Hacking the 2016 Election?" *Politico*, December 26, 2019. As of December 27, 2019:
https://www.politico.com/news/magazine/2019/12/26/
did-russia-really-hack-2016-election-088171